THE GUIDED DESIGN APPROACH

The Instructional Design Library
Volume 9

THE GUIDED DESIGN APPROACH

Charles E. Wales
West Virginia University
Morgantown, West Virginia
and
Robert A. Stager
University of Windsor
Windsor, Ontario, Canada

Danny G. Langdon
Series Editor

Educational Technology Publications
Englewood Cliffs, New Jersey 07632

Library of Congress Cataloging in Publication Data

Wales, Charles E
    The guided design approach.

    (The Instructional design library; v. no. 9)
    Bibliography: p.
    1. Programmed instruction. 2. Individualized
instruction. I. Stager, Robert A., joint author.
II. Title. III. Series.
LB1028.46.W34   371.39'442   77-27457
ISBN 0-87778-113-3

Printed in the United States of America.

Library of Congress Catalog Card Number:
77-27457.

International Standard Book Number:
0-87778-113-3.

First Printing: February, 1978.

FOREWORD

Be prepared to work through this instructional design. As the authors clearly state, the dynamics of Guided Design cannot be fully appreciated unless you participate in the simulation—just reading the book is not enough. They are to be commended for this approach, as well as the fine explanation and illustrations they provide.

Although Guided Design is a relatively new instructional design, the Resources section will more than adequately demonstrate that it is becoming widely accepted. I am particularly delighted to see that it speaks to one of those areas of learning with which we have traditionally had great difficulty —decision-making. It seems to me that since Guided Design does address itself to one of those seemingly "intangible" areas of learning, it should help to dispel the notion that instructional technology does not lend itself to "higher order skills." If Guided Design does only half the things the authors write about in the Outcomes section, then this is an instructional design worthy of your attention.

In a relatively short book, the authors have given a great deal of clear explanation, adequate examples, plenty of practice, and excellent guidelines on development.

Danny G. Langdon
Series Editor

PREFACE

Guided Design is an educational strategy that makes it possible for teachers to simultaneously accomplish two goals which have stubbornly resisted integration: (1) teaching subject matter, and (2) developing the decision-making skills required to apply what has been learned to the solution of real-world problems. With Guided Design, the teacher models professional reasoning and shows students how what they study can be used to make better decisions. A by-product of this process is increased motivation, which improves students' retention of subject matter.

Teachers who adopt Guided Design know that teaching is not just art based on the science of psychology, but *form*. Guided Design provides a form which allows the teacher to mediate, temporarily, between the student and the professional decision-maker. Through carefully drawn examples, the teacher helps the student experience the freedom of effective decision-making along with the responsibilities that this freedom entails. The teacher brings together the neophyte and the master so that one can see the judgments of the other.

Education, as it is defined today, supports a narrow viewpoint which limits both the form and scope of learning. It is true that education has to do with subject matter and achievement, but the legitimate range should be as Carl Rogers defined it, exercise for the whole person; memorization, yes, but application too, through both single-answer and open-ended problems. To know whether what has been learned is of value, the students must have not only some concept of a standard by which to judge, but also experience in making judgments. And just as what is studied grows in sophistication, so too should the knowledge of how to apply and evaluate.

To fully comprehend the ideas and works of others, students must be tuned in to their own impulses and confront others' thoughts by direct engagement and involvement. They must learn what questions to ask, what questions not to ask, and when to ask. To learn in a meaningful way, they must teach themselves. The teacher can anticipate their problems, their questions, their concerns, but no teacher can learn for a student. The sense of struggle must be with the student; the teacher can only provide the leading questions which prompt appropriate answers until emancipation occurs. The teacher is not an intellectual surgeon planting a Pacemaker in the student's brain, but rather a midwife who assists in the delivery of a free mind: independent but capable of commitment, playful, serious, adaptive, creative, an endurable human being in a tolerable world.

Within the structure of Guided Design, each student is free to inquire, think, and express a viewpoint subject only to the inner checks of reason and conscience—learning in the process that an autonomous agent must assume responsibility for acts and conduct, as well as ideas; learning the place of empathy, moral judgments, and the time to subordinate personal interests to the needs of others; and learning the role that continued study plays in better decision-making.

The ideas described in this book have been adopted by teachers in a variety of disciplines, including the humanities (for example, philosophy, drama, English), the social sciences (history, urban studies, international relations), natural sciences (chemistry, physics, biology), mathematics, engineering, business, technology, education, professional work (counseling and rehabilitation, nursing, veterinary pharmacology, dentistry, wildlife management), and in multidisciplinary studies. Although these ideas were originally applied by college teachers, they are applicable to all levels of education; and teachers who use Guided Design work in high schools, universities, continuing education, and business training programs.

Space does not permit us to thank each of the people who made an important contribution to the development of Guided Design, but the list includes teachers from the many disciplines listed above who developed Guided Design projects and helped shape the concept with their feedback. It also includes the students and teaching assistants who gave their support while we learned how to use this approach more effectively. The Exxon Education Foundation deserves a share of the credit for their continuing financial support. In addition, we would like to thank Linda Stokes, whose tireless and dedicated work helped make this book a reality. And, finally, we thank Gene D'Amour, whose effort and constructive criticism helped make Guided Design a successful innovation.

C.E.W.
R.A.S.

CONTENTS

ABSTRACT

THE GUIDED DESIGN APPROACH

Guided Design is an educational strategy that makes it possible for teachers to simultaneously accomplish two goals which have resisted integration: (1) teaching subject matter, and (2) developing the decision-making skills required to apply what has been learned to the solution of real-world problems.

With Guided Design, the teacher models professional reasoning and shows students how what they study can be used to make better decisions. A by-product of this process is increased motivation, which improves the students' retention of subject matter.

THE GUIDED DESIGN APPROACH

I.

USE

Guided Design is a new educational strategy, part system, part attitude. It reshapes the traditional approach to education by having students, working in small groups, attack open-ended problems rather than masses of cold information. It is based on the conviction that the student who works through an ascending order of well-designed problems—the student who is actively seeking solutions to problems rather than passively assimilating knowledge—will emerge not only better educated but also far stronger intellectually.

The learning process in this Design revolves around students' efforts to devise solutions for a series of carefully designed open-ended problems. While there is no single correct answer to any of the problems, each requires students to put into play specific information and skills in order to develop a feasible solution. The teacher selects the problems according to the skills and subject matter the students should learn, and prepares written instruction-feedback material which guides them through a "model" solution.

The manner in which students deal with the problems is carefully organized. Each problem is broken down into a sequence of decision-making steps. Students must deal with each step in order and are not permitted to progress to a new step until they have adequately considered and dealt with the preceding one. Students work on these open-ended problems in class, in groups of from four to seven members, and it is as a group that they formulate their plan for tackling each step. As intended by the teacher in the selection and sequencing of the problem, the group quickly discovers that certain information and skills are needed in order to make appropriate decisions. These needs have been anticipated by the preparation of a library of materials—traditional and programmed texts, reference books, audio-tapes, etc., which students are expected to study outside of class.

The solution of a given open-ended Guided Design problem may take only one week of class time or as much as five weeks. During this period of time, the students are expected to study and learn the same amount of subject matter that would normally have been considered in a "traditional" class. Tests on this material are given in the usual way. However, the students' motivation to learn is improved because at least part of the subject matter is required to produce an effective solution to the problem chosen by the teacher. Thus, this information is always brought back to the group to provide optimum conditions for group problem-solving, with its give-and-take of ideas, insights, and opinions.

When the group has decided upon its action for the decision-making step under consideration, it is given written feedback material, prepared in advance by the teacher. The material presents possible decisions the group may have reached at this point in its problem-solving, elaborating upon the strengths and weaknesses of each. After the students compare the pros and cons of their decision with those of the professional, they are allowed to advance to the next step in the problem.

By focusing on both decision-making and the acquisition of knowledge, Guided Design brings knowledge alive as the tool of an active mind seeking orderly solutions to complex problems. The open-ended nature of Guided Design problems and the stress on group problem-solving brings this approach even closer to "real-life" experience, where few problems are susceptible to a single solution, and where many different opinions and values must be considered and reconciled in the decision-making process. In sum, students not only acquire knowledge within the discipline under this approach, but also develop their ability to learn on their own, think logically, gather the information they need to make intelligent decisions, make value judgments, and communicate their ideas to others.

The concept of Guided Design was developed at West Virginia University in 1969 as a better way to teach engineering students. However, it quickly became apparent that it could be adopted by many—perhaps most—disciplines. The following year it was put to use in an undergraduate program in chemical engineering and a graduate program in counseling and rehabilitation. At WVU it is now used in 18 different departments, including civil engineering, counseling and guidance, drama, philosophy, wildlife management, curriculum and instruction, geography, and nursing. It also serves as the basis for a new interdisciplinary course on the nature of evidence, which draws elements from the sciences, social sciences, and humanities, including philosophy, anthropology, chemistry, history, physics, geology, biology, political science, psychology, and English.

The spread of this Design outside of West Virginia has been accelerated by a program sponsored by the Exxon Education Foundation, which had offered grants to faculty who wanted to adopt one of four innovations, including this Design. By 1976, this approach was in use in ten education colleges; five business programs; in the physical and natural sciences; in engineering; multidisciplinary studies; in the social sciences at eleven colleges; and in professional schools of veterinary medicine and in dentistry. It has also been used in high school classes and for training programs in business and industry. Thus, there appear to be no special limitations to the application of this approach.

Most of the adoptions of Guided Design have been in a single course, but there have been two, more elaborate, applications. One of these is in an *undergraduate* chemical engineering program, where it is used in one course each semester in the freshman and sophomore years. By the end of the sophomore year, the structure disappears and students move on in the junior year to one-page problem statements and finally to an in-house senior internship program.

At the *graduate* level, students in a two-year counseling and rehabilitation program begin using Guided Design in the second semester, where a six-credit course is offered. The following semester involves a supervised practicum, and the final semester is an internship in the field. Thus, Guided Design suits the needs of students at many different levels; the prime difference between undergraduate and graduate students is how quickly they develop decision-making skills and how soon the structure is withdrawn.

To sum up, Guided Design is an educational strategy that makes it possible for teachers to simultaneously accomplish two goals which have stubbornly resisted integration: (1) teaching subject matter, and (2) developing the decision-making skills required to apply what has been learned outside of class to the solution of real-world problems. With Guided Design, the teacher models professional reasoning and shows students how the material they study can be used to make better decisions. Six years of data show that an important by-product of this process is increased motivation, which improves the students' retention of subject matter and results in better grades.

II.

OPERATIONAL DESCRIPTION

Guided Design is based on our belief that teachers have something much more important to give their students than just information. That something is a model of how an intelligent human being makes a decision. A few people misinterpret this belief and assume that subject matter has no importance in a Guided Design course. Nothing could be further from the truth. In most cases, the same amount of subject matter is studied and learned as in a traditional course. However, the students study and learn this material outside of class. In the classroom, they spend most of their time working through projects. To integrate these activities, each project is organized around the subject matter (studied at home) during the period of time the students need to complete their project work in class.

Some people define teaching as a performance by someone who captures, holds, and directs the attention of students. They see the teacher as an actor who mediates between the script and the audience. Guided Design does provide a stage for the teacher's performance, but it is as a consultant, a thinking professional, and not as the actor center stage in the classroom. Director, coach, or manager are apt titles, but not actor. The script, which the teacher prepared, is in the hands of the students. If these roles appeal to you, then you should find Guided Design a compatible innovation.

In a Guided Design class the teacher moves from group to group, listening, asking leading questions, and encouraging students to participate in the decision-making process. The teacher also controls the flow of the Feedback-Instruction pages (see below) because students sometimes have a tendency to try to short-cut the decision-making process and ask for a Feedback page before they have demonstrated an appropriate level of thinking.

The best way we know to introduce you to the operation of a Guided Design class is to demonstrate how such a class might operate. The example we have chosen is a project used by many teachers on the first day of class, "The Fishing Trip: An Introduction to the Process of Decision-Making." Before you begin reading about the class operation, we suggest you stop long enough to create a mental picture of who and where you are. Visualize yourself as a student at the first day of class. You have just entered the room where 30 to 40 other students sit in chairs which can be moved. The purpose of this first class is to introduce you and the other students to (a) the course, and (b) the process of decision-making in a Guided Design format.

The first few minutes of this Guided Design course are not particularly unusual. The teacher makes appropriate introductions and passes out a syllabus for the course which explains the general pattern of operation, the grading plan, and other details which are pertinent. Then the new pattern begins.

When the introduction is completed, the teacher passes out the first sheet of the Fishing Trip and asks each student to read it and individually complete the "First Exercise." When all are done, the teacher organizes the students into groups of four to seven people and passes out the next sheet, which includes the "Second Exericse" and Instruction A. When a group indicates they have completed their discussion of the question in A, the teacher checks the secretary's list. If it looks like the group has done some thinking, the next page is passed out, Feedback A and Instruction B. This process is repeated with each step until each groups completes the project. (Note: This introductory project takes a little over one-hour to complete; the subject-matter based projects used in the course generally take much longer.)

Now we'd like you to work through the "Fishing Trip" project as if you were a student in this class. Don't just read Figures 1 to 10—read each question and try to respond to it. Of course, you will not have the advantage of a group to contribute ideas and debate those that are suggested. But play the game as best you can. After you reach a decision, read the Feedback which presents one view of what might have been decided. When you complete this reading assignment, we hope you will seriously consider trying Guided Design in your class.

The Fishing Trip: An Introduction to the Process of Decision-Making*

Figure 1

INTRODUCTION

Many of you have probably gone on an automobile trip only to have the car break down on the highway. Although this can be inconvenient and annoying, help is usually within walking distance and there is little danger involved. In contrast, imagine the problem you might have if you had a breakdown while out in a boat on a fishing trip in the Gulf of Mexico. That's the situation we want you to deal with in this one-hour project. You will be asked to participate in this situation in two ways. First, there is an *individual exercise* in which you are asked to rank a list of items. Second, you are asked to work as *part of a team* to explore the best way to deal with the problem.

THE SETTING

It was the first week in August when four friends set out on an overnight fishing trip in the Gulf of Mexico. Everything went well the first day—the sea was calm, they caught fish, and later camped out on a lovely little island. However, during the night a very strong wind pulled the anchor free, drove their boat ashore, and the pounding waves broke the propeller. Although there were oars in the boat, the motor was useless.

A quick review of the previous day's journey showed that the group was about 60 miles from the nearest habitated land. The small deserted island they were on had a few scrub trees and bushes, but no fresh water. They knew from their portable am-fm radio that the weather would be hot and dry, with daytime temperatures expected to be over 100°F the rest of the week. They were all dressed in light clothing but each had a windbreaker for the cool evenings. They agreed that whatever happened they would stick together.

The families back on shore expected the group to return from their trip that evening and would surely report them missing when they didn't show up. However, they realized that it might take time for someone to find them because they went out further than anyone might have expected.

While some members of the group were quite concerned about this predicament, there was no panic. To help keep the group calm, one of

(Continued on Next Page)

Figure 1 (Continued)

the group, Jim, suggested that, just to be safe, they inventory the food and equipment available to them. "It might be several days before we are safe," Jim said, "and I think we should prepare for that." Kate, Tom and Ann agreed and their effort produced the list of items given in Figure 2.

*Reprinted with permission from the book *Guided Design*, published at West Virginia University by C. E. Wales and R. A. Stager, 1977.

Figure 2

FIRST EXERCISE–INDIVIDUAL WORK

After the list was complete, Jim suggested that each person independently rank these items according to the importance of each item to the survival of the group. Each member of the group agreed to do this. Without discussing the problem with anyone else, they would individually rank the items from number "1," for the item which was most important, to number "14," the item least important to survival.

(We would like you to assume that you are a member of this group and individually rank these items on the form provided. *Write your list of numbers in the space marked Column A.*)

Items Available	A	Z	B	Y	X
Each person has					
a. one windbreaker					
b. one poncho					
c. one sleeping bag					
d. one pair of sunglasses					
The boat contains					
e. a cooler with two bottles of pop per person and some ice.					
f. one large flashlight					
g. one first-aid kit					
h. fishing equipment					
i. matches, rope, and a few tools					
j. one compass mounted on the boat					
k. two rear-view mirrors which can be removed from the boat.					
l. one "official" navigational map of the Gulf area where you are					
m. one salt shaker (full)					
n. one bottle of liquor					

Column

Figure 3

SECOND EXERCISE–GROUP DECISION-MAKING
Form groups of four to seven people.

Introduction

The material you are about to use is concerned with decision-making, a basic intellectual process which makes it possible for each of us to face and solve new problems. This material is organized in an "Instruction-Feedback" pattern so you can participate in the solution of the problem. Each instruction presents a question the group on the island raised about one step in the decision-making process. We suggest that each member of your group read each Instruction, *discuss it with your team, decide on a group response*, and then compare the decision with the printed Feedback which your teacher will provide. This Feedback offers a summary of what your group has probably discussed and presents the decision made by the group on the island. You should realize that the purpose of the printed Feedback is to allow everyone to compare their reasoning with that of other people. No one should feel that they have to accept any of these decisions.

Each group should *appoint a secretary to record* the decisions made by his or her teammates. When the group feels they have completed their answer to the Instruction, ask the teacher to come to the group to check the work or have the secretary take the record to the teacher. If the teacher believes the work is acceptable, the secretary will receive copies of the Feedback and the next Instruction to give to the group. If the work is not yet acceptable, the teacher may ask questions to stimulate further thinking.

Instruction A –The Problem

When the group on the island finished their work on the list of items, Tom, who was visibly shaken, spoke up. "I'm not sure that what we have done so far makes any sense. I'm really worried!"

"Do you want to make a group list?" Jim asked.
"No," Tom said, "I think we should *talk about what we are going to do about our problem*."

(Assume you are the group on the island and discuss what you would do about this problem.)

Figure 4

Feedback A

The four friends had quite an animated discussion about what to do. Some of their ideas were to:

Row to shore or
Stay on the island and
Gather wood
Build a fire
Ration food and water
Catch fish
Build a shelter
Take the mirrors off the boat

Instruction B—Identify the Problem

Tom, who had now calmed down, spoke again. "I think we're making progress now, but I'm *not* sure we're on the right track. I get the feeling that all the ideas we listed should be called POSSIBLE SOLUTIONS—we talked about *what we should do to solve our problem, BUT NOT ABOUT THE PROBLEM THESE SOLUTIONS ARE SUPPOSED TO SOLVE.*"

"Tom's right," Kate said, "We can't generate intelligent possible solutions unless we know exactly what the problem is we face. Let's see if we can *agree on the problem we want to solve.*"

The others agreed and they proceeded with this task.

Figure 5

Feedback B

This time the group came up with a list of what they thought were potential problems. They said the problem is:

1. We're stuck on this island.
2. The propeller is broken.
3. Survival.

Instruction C—Identify the Problem

"Wait," Jim said, "I think we've got problems mixed with causes. It's a subtle difference, but an important one. The broken propeller and the fact that we're stuck here got us into trouble—they caused our problem, but the immediate problem we face is survival."

"I agree," Ann said, "but survival is too broad a word. We can't generate good solutions unless we *pinpoint* the problem that threatens our lives. I think we've got to define the most basic problem we face. *What is the specific problem that is most likely to threaten our survival?*"

Figure 6

Feedback C

After a brief discussion, the group agreed that the immediate threat to their lives was either starvation, sunburn, or dehydration. Then they decided that they could get out of the sun and avoid a "burn." They could also eat fish so they wouldn't starve. But they had no source of fresh water. Thus, dehydration seemed to be the most serious problem and the one on which they should focus.

"It seems clear to me," Ann said, "that we have not only identified the problem we face, but stated the goal of our work as well, our *goal* is to stay alive by avoiding dehydration." The others agreed.

Instruction D–Facts, Assumptions, Constraints/Choose a Solution

"OK," Tom said, "our goal is to prevent dehydration. I suggest we pool what we know and list the facts, assumptions, and constraints which affect this goal."

"The *facts* are easy," Ann said. "We're stuck 60 miles from the nearest habitation where we can get help and it's going to be hot and dry during the day."

"Yes, and we can *assume* that our families will miss us and someone should be looking for us tomorrow," Kate added.

"And," Tom continued, "the *constraints* are that we have only the items on our list to work with plus the few trees, bushes, and the sand here on the island.

"Given this state of affairs," Jim added, "let's *make a list of the things we must avoid to forestall dehydration and then make our choice, either to stay on the island or to row to shore.*"

Figure 7

Feedback D

The group generated the following list. To avoid dehydration they would have to:

1. do as little exercise as possible
2. keep out of the sun and wind
3. eat nothing
4. avoid alcohol and salt

"I think we've got a good list," Tom said. "Now, let's see if we can use it to *choose the best possible solution.* Since our goal is to avoid dehydration, the question we must answer is, How can we best avoid dehydration? We have two options, stay or row to shore. Which should we do?" After a short discussion, the group agreed that staying on the island was the best possible solution because it would be easier to avoid dehydration if they could avoid the open water and the exercise involved in rowing the boat.

Instruction E—Analysis/Synthesis

"We've done a good job," Ann said, "and now is the proper time to use the list Jim had us develop earlier. Now is the time to *rank the items we have available.* Why don't we see if we can make more sense out of the list now that we know our goal is to prevent dehydration and the best possible solution is to stay here on the island."

"When we're done with our work on the list," Kate added, "I suggest we *synthesize our thinking into a short statement that represents our final plan.*" The group agreed and together they proceeded with their new ranking of the items.

(Each person should write the numbers selected by the group in Column B—leave Column Y blank for now. Please do not change the work you did earlier in Column A.)

Figure 8

Feedback E

The result of this Instruction is your ranked list of items.

The group summarized their thinking in the following way. Given all this information, the group's final decision was to stay on the island and wait for rescue. They would protect themselves from dehydration, from the sun and the hot, dry air, by wearing the sunglasses and the windbreakers and developing a shady shelter with the ponchos and sleeping bags. The mirror, flashlight, and a fire would be used to signal rescuers. The pop and ice water would be used as needed, but no food or liquor would be consumed.

Information F—Evaluation

The group implemented their plan quite effectively and with excellent results. Everyone was in good shape when, three days later, a search plane came near enough to the island for them to signal with the mirror. A few hours more and a Coast Guard vessel came into view and the four friends were soon aboard enjoying a sweet sip of water. After they had rested, the Captain dropped in to ask them how they had survived in such good shape. The group told him about their decision-making and the lists they had prepared.

"I know a good deal about survival," the Captain said. "Why don't I rank the list of items and you can check your work against mine."

The group agreed and the Captain gave the following explanation.
(Write these numbers to the right, in Column X.)

1. (k) *Two rear-view mirrors*
    "The best way to avoid dehydration is to be rescued, so your first concern should be to develop a signal system. Because a search is most likely to take place in daylight, the mirrors are of prime importance—with a mirror you can generate a beam of light that can be seen a long way. You might get as much as 6 million candle power on a bright day. The chance of being rescued is very high if all you have is a mirror and sunshine.

(Continued on Next Page)

Figure 8 (Continued)

2. (f) *One large flashlight*
"To complete your signaling potential, you should count on the flashlight. With the light and the mirror you can signal at night as well as in the daytime.

3. (i) *Matches, rope, and tools*
"Matches plus parts removed from the boat and/or gasoline provide another signaling device, a fire. The flame at night or smoke during the day should provide an excellent signal. In addition, the rope can help you create a daytime shelter.

4. (a) *Windbreaker*
"Your second concern should be to slow down dehydration by reducing both respiration and perspiration. To be effective at this task you should put yourself in the place of those who know how to survive a hot, dry climate—the animals you have seen over and over again in Walt Disney movies and on "Wild Kingdom" TV shows. Animals, who live in a hot, dry climate, survive by staying out of the sun and limiting their activity. You can do the equivalent by staying quietly in the shade to reduce respiration and insulating yourself from the hot, dry air with the windbreakers. This will increase your survival time significantly.

5. (b) *One poncho each*
6. (c) *One sleeping bag each*
"These two items are considered together because both, in combination with the rope, can be used to create enough shade to reduce the temperature by up to 20°. This is an important reduction which can prolong life. You might also be able to use the poncho to create a solar still and produce some fresh water.

7. (d) *One pair of sunglasses each*
"By the second day, the intense sunlight can produce serious eye problems, equivalent to snow blindness. The shade provided by the shelter will help, but sunglasses offer additional safety.

8. (e) *The cooler of ice and pop*
"This amount of liquid will not offset the inevitable effects of dehydration. Thus, there is no point in rationing the pop and

(Continued on Next Page)

Figure 8 (Continued)

water. Instead, it should be consumed when you are thirsty, on the first day, so you can keep a clear head as you make the important decisions that will affect your survival.

9. (g) *First-aid kit*
"This kit would be of value if anyone were hurt, but the island is likely to be a very healthy place because it is so dry. Even if someone were cut, they would not be likely to bleed because their blood is dehydrating and thickening.

Items of Little Value
10. (l) Navigation map
11. (j) Compass
"These two items are of value only if the group tries to row to shore, which is likely to be a fatal mistake. If no one were looking for you, this might be a viable option, but it is not in this situation. You should use the map for a sun shade, to build a fire, or as toilet paper.

12. (h) Fishing equipment
13. (n) Liquor
14. (m) Salt Shaker
"The fishing equipment could be used to catch food, but the activity would dehydrate you even faster. In addition, eating requires water for digestion so you would accelerate dehydration by eating.
"The liquor may be liquid, but in this case it's liquid death. Alcohol is a dehydrating agent so if you want to go fast, but happy, you should drink the liquor. It might better be used to cool the skin.
"Salt also acts as a dehydrating agent. You do not need to replace the salt in your blood, it is already too salty because you are dehydrating. Therefore, avoid the salt."

At this point Kate interrupted with a question. "I understand and agree with what you've said, but some of us felt that fixing a shelter was more important than worrying about rescue because we knew you wouldn't even begin to look for us until the next day."

(Continued on Next Page)

Figure 8 (Continued)

"That's a good point," the Captain responded, "and I couldn't argue if you switched the list around with shelter first. The point is to avoid dehydration by either reducing it or getting off the island."

Instruction F—Evaluation

"The success of your plan was demonstrated when you were rescued in such good shape," the Captain said, "But let's see how well your choices stacked up against my evaluation. To determine how your group did compared to my advice, I suggest you score your work in the following way:

First Exercise—Individual Scores

1. "Subtract to obtain the *'absolute difference'* $A-X$, the difference between Column A (your individual ranking) and my ranking (X). Write the result in Column Z.

2. "Each person should add all the 'difference' numbers in their Column Z to get a total for their work.

3. "Calculate an average individual score for your group: the sum of the Z results divided by the number in your group.

Second Exercise—Group Decision-Making Score

4. "Subtract to obtain the *absolute difference* $B-X$, the difference between Column B (the group ranking) and my ranking (X). Write the result in Column Y.

5. "Add the 'difference' numbers in Column Y to get a total score for the group ranking.

Figure 9

Feedback F

The Captain suggested that to see the evolution of their scores, the group compare the average individual score (Z) with the group decision-making score (Y). The point was well made because the four friends could see that their group score (Y) was lower (or closer to the Captain's evaluation) than the individual score (Z).

The Captain summed up the work with the following points.

1. "The more you know about the key elements involved in a problem, the more successful you are likely to be at finding a workable solution. For instance, in this problem, the more you know about dehydration the more likely you are to survive. In other words, the things you study and learn, whether in school or out, can help you be a more effective problem-solver.

2. "A group can usually arrive at a better decision than an individual, especially if the people in the group understand how to work together to share what they know and what they think.

3. "Your decision-making work is likely to be much more effective if you know which steps to take and how to use each step. If you are skilled at this process you are less likely to commit one of the classic errors, such as generating possible solutions before you identify the problem to be solved. After you properly define both the problem and the goal, you are also in a much better position to decide what information you need to proceed intelligently.

"Perhaps I should stress," the Captain continued, "that identifying the problem and stating the goal are extremely important steps in the solution of any problem. If you have not done these steps properly, you are not likely to produce the best solution; you may miss possible solutions which should not be missed or perform an excellent analysis of the wrong problem. An example of this occurred in the early development of the U.S. space program when a problem similar to the following was posed.

(Continued on Next Page)

Figure 9 (Continued)

Find a material which will withstand a temperature of 14,000°F for five minutes.

Of course, this problem was related to the re-entry of a space capsule and the enormous amount of heat generated during the process.

"A great deal of time and money was wasted trying to solve this problem because there was no known material which would withstand the required temperature. Finally, someone realized that they were trying to solve the wrong problem. The new problem was stated as follows.

Find a way to protect a capsule and the person inside during re-entry.

This problem was solved very quickly with the ablation system now in use.

"The problem you faced on the island was very similar to this re-entry problem," the Captain said. "If you focus on getting to shore and not the real problem of dehydration, then you are likely to miss the solution that results in survival."

Epilog
Through this problem we have tried to indicate in a very brief way that many steps are required in the solution of an open-ended problem. In the more involved problems which follow, you will be asked to perform these steps, learning as you go how to perform them with greater and greater skill. As you work on each problem, you will be expected to use what you already know and to learn new fundamental principles which are required to produce the desired result. In this sense, you will be operating exactly like a problem solver in the real world, who commands a broad background but must often search out new information and skills to produce the best solution.

Before we move on to the next problem, it would be well for you to review the steps we have performed here. Although the order in which these steps are used may vary from problem to problem, the steps themselves are an important key to successful work. Try to list the

(Continued on Next Page)

Figure 9 (Continued)

steps we have used, then check your list against our "Steps in Decision-Making."

Debriefing: Congratulations!

You have just completed your first Guided Design class. If you decide you'd like to try this approach in a class you are presently teaching, you should reproduce enough copies of our Fishing Trip project so each student can have one set. *You have our permission to do this, as long as you give proper credit.* This material should not be collated, because it will be passed out one page at a time. (Note: these "debriefing" paragraphs should be deleted from the students' copies.)

If you decide to adopt the Guided Design style for your class, this "Introduction to Decision-Making" is extremely important, because it helps the students understand the process which will be a prime focus of their work throughout the course. However, we should point out that this introduction has one unique feature which is not present in a typical Guided Design project; that is the scoring at the end of the project, where the students compare their solution with that of the captain; the usual pattern used in Guided Design does not include this type of comparison and scoring.

Even if you don't plan to convert your course to Guided Design, you may find this project valuable because of what it can contribute to your students' abilities. For example, this material would be particularly appropriate in any course where the teacher already devotes some time to discussion activities. In fact, if you choose to teach the decision-making process in such a class with this material, we expect you will find the quality of the students' discussion improved.

III.

DESIGN FORMAT

In the past 30 years, people have developed computers and other devices which technologically extend their innate ability to make decisions. But even with this new power, decision-making is still a trial and error process which produces its share of dinosaurs. You have only to look around to observe the results. Part of the problem is the complex nature of the decision-making process—it depends on data that is always limited in some way, on the rational use of the process steps, on the personal characteristics of the participants, and on interpersonal relationships such as cooperation, competition, manipulation, and domination. Our experience indicates that the likelihood of successful and effective decision-making can be increased significantly by helping people learn the steps in this process and providing supervised practice with some technique such as Guided Design.

The design format of this new strategy can be described in a variety of ways, and we plan to use several approaches here to illustrate what is involved in developing and operating a course. First, we show that development begins with the subject matter, which is used as the base for the preparation of a Guided Design project. We continue with an explanation of the different ways in which teachers have modified course plans to incorporate these projects.

Next, we illustrate the role a study guide can play in helping the students learn subject matter and, then, the components included in the study guide for the Guided Design project itself. The use of student project leaders is also explained. Finally, the format of Guided Design is examined in terms of both the goals it is designed to achieve and the psychological principles used as a base for the design.

Although the concept of Guided Design is based on our belief that teachers have something much more important to give their students than just information, subject matter still plays an important role in a Guided Design course. In fact, in most cases, the same amount of subject matter is studied and learned with Guided Design as in a traditional course. However, the students study and learn this material outside of class; in the classroom they spend most of their time working through three (to five) Guided Design projects per term. To integrate these activities, each Guided Design project is organized around the subject matter studied at home.

The importance of this integration of subject matter and project work is well illustrated by the next two paragraphs which present our advice to those who plan to write a Guided Design project.

1. Although the starting point for your work on a Guided Design project might well be a favorite open-ended problem, you must eventually relate that problem to some portion of the subject matter you expect to teach. Therefore, we suggest you begin your work by selecting the subject matter you expect the students to learn in some 1 to 4 week segment of your course.

2. Choose a situation which involves this subject matter and *outline your project* before you begin to write. Make sure that most, if not all, of the decision-making steps are included in your outline.

was used to build a cognitive base for the creative work which followed.

Some teachers have gone much further with Guided Design. In the freshman engineering program at WVU, for example, half the decision-making work in a sequence of two courses is presented as Guided Design. Graduate students in reading education can take three courses designed to help them function more effectively as professionals in the school system. In contrast, teachers in the School of Nursing developed one Guided Design course which provides their graduate students with an opportunity to integrate the subject matter studied in two other conventional courses taught during the same semester. Other teachers have developed even more extensive decision-making experiences. In a graduate counseling and rehabilitation program, for example, Guided Design was used to create a six-credit course which models professional practice and shows the need for both interaction skills and background knowledge. This course is followed by a practicum and an internship.

In the chemical engineering program at WVU, teachers revamped the undergraduate program to include decision-making in at least one course each semester. Some Guided Design is used in the sophomore year, but this quickly gives way to other forms of decision-making, including a 10-credit design course in the senior year, in which the students are organized as a corporate design team. This preplanned focus on decision-making over a period of three years, plus increased emphasis on written and oral reports, has helped these students develop skills which are highly prized by business and industry.

Although a Guided Design course can be organized around a textbook, and the set of projects prepared by the teacher, other teaching-learning aids may be required. Our experience has shown that some textbooks are written so lectures are necessary; the students have great difficulty handling text material without these lectures. However, many teachers have already demonstrated that self-study of the *subject matter* can be supported by carefully selecting the textbook, by adding objectives, notes, or a study guide, or by adopting the Personalized System of Instruction, programmed instruction, or audio-tutorial instruction. One of these approaches, therefore, may be a necessary addition to a Guided Design course.

We have found that a *study guide for the Guided Design project* can also be very useful. In this guide we try to relate the project work to the students' lives, give an outline of the project, describe the basis for the students' grades, and provide objectives for the students' decision-making work. The first page of a sample study guide for the "Educational Experience" project is shown in Figure 12. The project outline given in a study guide has proved to be of particular importance because students usually have had little decision-making training and they feel much more comfortable if they have some idea of what is about to happen. In addition, their decision-making work is unnaturally fragmented from one class to the next, over a period as long as four weeks, and the outline helps them remember where they have been and see where they are going.

Another aid which should be included in the study guide is a set of objectives for the decision-making work. The sample objectives presented in Figure 13, from the educational experience project, describe what the students should be able to do by the time they complete the project. In this case, the objectives are based on material presented in the project itself, such as Maslow's (1968) Need Hierarchy, which is mentioned in Objective A, and on the outside reading, which is a reprint of an article on the use of psychology to improve teaching practices.

Figure 12

The Design of an Educational Experience:
Study Guide

During the next two class periods you will work through a project that models the way in which a team of people approach the task of designing an "optimum" educational experience. We expect this project will be of particular interest to you if you are presently involved in "education," because you are undoubtedly concerned about what IS happening and what SHOULD BE happening. Even if you are not involved in formal education these ideas should be of value because your life will surely involve teaching other people in some way: children, friends, fellow workers, etc.

The steps used by the group as they work their way through this problem are the following:

A. Identify One of the Problems of Education.
B. State the Goals of the Educational Design Work.
C. Generate Possible Solutions for the Decision-Making Goal.
D. Apply Theoretical Constraints to a Preliminary Evaluation.
E. Generate Possible Solutions for the Subject Matter/Values Goals.
F. Gather Information for the Analysis-Synthesis-Evaluation Work.

Your *grade* on this project may be based on such things as:

1. Attendance and participation in the classroom decision-making work.
2. Homework and quizzes based on the objectives given later in this study guide.
3. Your parallel project.

Figure 13

The Design of an Educational Experience:
Objectives

After completing this project, students should be able to satisfy the following objectives:

(A) *Identify One of the Problems of Education.*
     Apply the items in the Need Hierarchy to given situations.

(B) *State the Goals of the Educational Design Work.*
     Use the three goals presented in this project, (1) Knowledge, (2) Values, (3) Decision-Making to evaluate specific programs.

(C) *Generate Possible Solutions for Goal 3.*
     Describe the pattern of work which would exist in classes designed to develop decision-making abilities.

(D) *Apply Theoretical Constraints to a Preliminary Evaluation.*
     Use the five Psychological Principles presented in both this project and the reading assignment to evaluate a given teaching-learning-testing approach for Goal 3.

(E) *Generate Possible Solutions for Goals 1 and 2.*
     Use the five Psychological Principles presented in both this project and the reading assignment to select an optimum mix of teaching-learning-testing activities for Goals 1 and 2.

(F) *Gather Information for the Analysis-Synthesis-Evaluation Work.*
     (1) Describe the good and bad features of the educational design proposed in this project.
     (2) Apply these design ideas to another course and evaluate the pattern of operation.

A second component we recommend for a study guide is a "Parallel Project" assignment. This assignment allows students to have an individualized decision-making experience equivalent to that which they had in class with their group. For instance, the sample project illustrated here models the steps used by a group of alumni, students, and teachers as they approach the task of designing an optimum educational experience. The parallel project assignment, which is shown in Figure 14, asks the students to apply equivalent steps to a course they have had.

In a freshman engineering class, where the sudents have worked through a project to make a building accessible to a man in a wheelchair, the parallel project is to examine three campus buildings and recommend ways to make them accessible. In a philosophy class, where the project modeled the work of an analytic philosopher who defined the word "science," the parallel project assignment is to use the same steps to define another word, such as "alive," or "human being," or "cheating." In general, the outline of decision-making steps given in this assignment matches the steps used in the classroom project.

Some Guided Design projects model the whole decision-making process, including the synthesis of "A" solution (not "THE" solution). Others stop short of a solution, so the students are free to make their own choice. In either case, teachers should encourage their students to disagree with the printed solution at any point. In some projects, the students may actually strike out on their own probing for a totally unique solution and use the printed material simply as a guide to the decision-making steps. In other words, much flexibility can be built into the operation of a Guided Design class, and we hope that teachers allow for this.

One of the other techniques we have found to be productive in a Guided Design class is to select one student to serve

Figure 14

The Design of an Educational Experience:
Parallel Project

Recommended Procedure for the Parallel Project
and Your Report

The parallel project we would like you to undertake is *the evaluation of a course you have taken using what you learned in this project as the basis for the work.* During the past year you have surely taken one course which may or may not have satisfied all three of the goals listed in this project: Knowledge, Values, and Decision-Making. *Identify this course and use it as the basis for the following steps.*

1. *Identify an Educational Problem*
   a. State whether or not Knowledge, Values, and Decision-Making were taught in your course. In other words, (1) did you study subject matter and values, and (2) were you *taught* how to make decisions (being *asked* to make decisions is not the same as being *taught* how to make them).
   b. Does a problem exist in your course? Use the Need Hierarchy given in the project to explain your answer. If you think goals should be added or removed, say so.

2. *Gather Information*
   List the teaching-learning-testing activities actually used in your course to achieve the
   a. subject matter and/or value goals.
   b. decision-making goal.

3. *Preliminary Evaluation*
   Use the five Psychological Principles given in this project to evaluate the teaching-learning-testing activities actually used in your course.

---

as the "project leader." This person keeps complete notes on what the group has decided to do, and he or she confers with the teacher to determine if the group is ready to move ahead. (The other members of the team keep a brief "log" of their progress so they don't lose track of where they are in the solution.) When the students reach the end of a project, the leader is allowed one week to write a report about the group's decision. The other members of the group have this week to prepare individual reports on the parallel project assignment. This work is done at home while the class continues with subject matter testing or a new project. Since the students do not know each other, the teacher usually appoints the leader for the first project, the others who follow can be selected by the group.

As you would expect, the format of Guided Design is a direct function of the goals chosen as a base for the design. These goals are:

- *Goal 1—Knowledge of Facts and Concepts*
  The student studies the facts and concepts appropriate to the course, the discipline, and the open-ended problems under consideration.

- *Goal 2—Aware of Values*
  The student studies the values, attitudes, beliefs, and feelings of other people which are relevant to the open-ended problems under consideration.

- *Goal 3—Decision-Making*
  The student works both independently and as part of a team to solve open-ended problems consciously using personal Knowledge and Value beliefs. In addition, the student learns by self-study, thinks independently, thinks logically, gathers, organizes and

uses the information learned to make decisions, communicates ideas, and uses the decision-making process including analysis, synthesis and evaluation.

To help students understand why a Guided Design class is organized around these three goals we present the triangle shown in Figure 15 and explain that to function as an independent, adaptive, creative, self-actualized human being, each person must have the ability to make decisions. This ability in turn is supported by both the background knowledge and the values of the individual. We point out that a decision based on knowledge alone or values alone is likely to be an unbalanced decision. To illustrate this, we describe the scientist or engineer who is often accused of ignoring values, and the humanist who, it is often claimed, bases decisions on values with insufficient concern for what is feasible. We might also add some politicians who appear to ignore both knowledge and values.

To implement these goals, the designer of a Guided Design course organizes the students' experience around Goal 3, a classroom effort to devise solutions for a series of carefully prepared open-ended problems. The teacher selects the problems according to the skills and subject matter the students should learn, and then prepares printed instruction-feedback material to guide the students through a "model" solution. With this printed material, the teacher brings together the neophyte and the master so that one can see the judgments of the other. The students work through each problem one step at a time, so they have a *slow-motion* experience in decision-making. The students play the role of a professional; they do the thinking, but they are not permitted to progress to a new step until they have adequately considered and dealt with the preceding one.

The values goal may be achieved in a variety of ways. In

Figure 15

The Self-Actualization Triangle

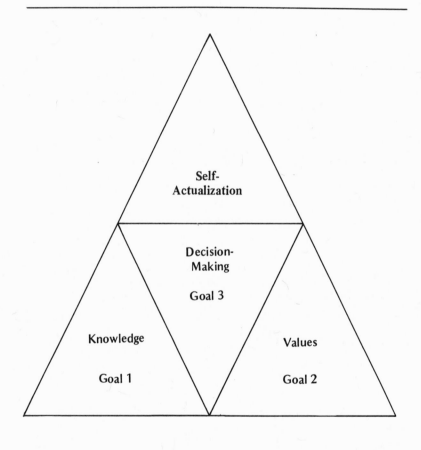

some classes, values are taught as part of the subject matter, so they play a natural role in the project work. In other classes, values, as such, as not "taught." However, it is likely that in such a class all of the open-ended problems the students solve will require them to make value judgments. In either case, it is the interaction in small groups which brings students face to face with different values—differences which have to be reconciled to arrive at a group decision. Value judgments are also modeled by both the printed Guided Design material and by the teacher who interacts with the students when they receive the next feedback-instruction page. So, values are openly displayed in class, where students can see how value judgments relate to the use of the subject matter and to realistic problems such as those they might one day face.

There are at least two ways in which Goal 1, the subject matter, can be related to the students' project work: what they learn outside of class can be used in the project to help them arrive at a better decision, or the use of the subject matter may follow the project so the students can examine how the decision was made. As an example of the latter, consider what happens in the multidisciplinary Nature of Evidence course. One of the early projects in this course models the way in which a chemist conducts an investigation. The students then study text material on both the scientific method and the use of lawful-deductive explanations. These concepts, in turn, are used by the students to examine the chemist's work to see if both techniques were, in fact, used.

In the other—more common—option, the subject matter is studied outside of class while the project work moves forward in class. These two components merge when the students realize that what they have learned can help them make a better decision. For example, in a freshman engineering class, the students use what they have learned about the first law of thermodynamics to design a system to move materials. In a theatre history course, the students design a set for Oedipus Rex using what they have learned about the Greek theatre.

The format of Guided Design is also a function of the five psychological principles used as a base for the design: guide, provide practice, evaluate and give feedback, motivate, and individualize. We can illustrate the way these principles affect the design by answering a series of five questions.

Question 1. "Does this teaching-learning approach *guide* the student's decision-making learning?"

Guiding the student is a prime focus of the Guided Design approach. The student's decision-making work in class is guided by printed Instruction-Feedback material which models the way in which a professional might attack the problem. The student also has guidance from the thinking of other students in the small group and from the teacher who manages the operation. Objectives, study guides, and the list of decision-making steps all provide further guidance for the student who works on class projects and prepares individual project reports.

We might point out that in a typical Guided Design class the students are not only allowed, but often required to redo tests and reports until an acceptable level of performance is achieved. Each round of testing or writing represents a form of guidance which prepares each student for the next attempt. Thus Guided Design does provide guidance, and in many ways.

Question 2. "Does Guided Design provide for *practice* with the decision-making process?"

The open-ended problem-solving which is the basis for Guided Design provides practice with both decision-making and value judgments. In class, students practice by discussing and presenting the group's decisions. Outside of class, they prepare individual project reports. Where parallel projects are assigned, the students practice the entire process of decision-making by independently solving an open-ended problem. Interaction within each group also provides important practice in dealing with a variety of values and helps students develop an openness to new ideas, sensitivity to the needs of others, and a willingness to share.

Question 3. "Does this teaching-learning approach *evaluate* the student's work and give *feedback*?"

As the students make decisions and value judgments in class, they get both evaluation and feedback from their classmates, the teacher, and the printed material. They also get evaluation and feedback on their thinking through the decision-making tests and project reports.

Question 4. "Does the Guided Design approach *motivate*?"

Motivation is built into the Guided Design approach in several ways. One is the open-ended problems used in class, which are chosen to motivate the students. Individual contributions are reinforced by the other members of the group. Parallel projects allow significant freedom and thus provide motivation by allowing each student to work on the project of his or her choice. The student is encouraged to succeed by retesting and through the opportunity to resubmit project reports until success is achieved.

Question 5. "Does this approach *individualize* the learning process?"

The Guided Design approach provides for individualization in a variety of ways. There is some degree of individualization in the classroom, where each group can move at its own pace. Within a group, each student can make an individual contribution and get individualized help on the decision-making work from "friends" or perhaps what might better be called "colleagues." Since students are allowed to rewrite both tests and reports, those who require more guidance and practice do in fact receive it.

These five psychological principles also affect the format of the subject matter part of this course, as illustrated below:

Guidance. To provide guidance the teacher should prepare both *objectives* and a *study guide.* Together these activities help the students organize their learning, provide for self-testing, and keep their efforts focused on relevant material. *Homework* assignments should be included because they provide guidance (as well as practice and feedback) and help students learn to pace their work. Homework is important too because it produces the response needed to insure that learning takes place. *Modeling* by way of sample problem solutions should be added because it is an important means of providing guidance to inexperienced people, both in solving single-answer problems and in displaying attitudes.

Practice. In many classes, practice and feedback take the form of a midsemester and final examination. This means students have a very limited opportunity to demonstrate what they have learned—these exams only sample what had been presented. This pattern can be improved measurably by the use of frequent, *competency-based tests* (Block, 1971), which pace the students' learning and allow them to restudy what is needed before they retest. In freshman engineering, for example, students are allowed to repeat examinations as often as required within a one-week time limit during the first semester and they can take each subject matter exam twice in the second semester. Required *homework* assignments provide the same desirable type of paced practice and help to build self-confidence.

Feedback. The only feedback some students get is graded midterm and final examinations. Their response all too often is to simply file these away because there is no reward for any further action. This pattern can be improved by the use of both *competency-based testing* and regular *homework* assignments because the students have a chance to correct learning errors and resubmit their work for further feedback.

Motivation. Some people express concern that a technique such as Guided Design eliminates almost all the lecturing in a class; lectures, after all, can be motivating. However, we know that too many students are motivated only by grades, not by lectures or by the material they study, and this is the wrong motivation. This situation can be improved by providing objectives, competency-based testing, and frequent feedback. But we can add *positive reinforcement, extra help* on studying and testing, and *meaningful work*, which might be defined as work which is related to the real world use of what is being studied. Each of these components can produce a significant improvement in the students' motivation to learn.

Individualization. If you adopt Guided Design, you may find it desirable and/or necessary to support the students' out of class study of the subject matter in the ways we have described. Some teachers do this by making regular homework assignments which are checked within the groups at the beginning of the next class period. For instance, in freshman engineering, where the students learn how to perform thermodynamic calculations, the project leaders are told to take whatever time is necessary, before they start their Guided Design work, to discuss the assigned homework problems with their group and to make sure that each member of the team understands how to solve the problems. The impact of this peer instruction is believed to be most significant.

The teachers in this freshman class provide subject matter help to any group or individual that needs it. Occasionally they may even give a brief lecture to the whole class to explain a point that is particularly troublesome. Great stress is put on helping the students learn to perform the algebraic calculations required to work with the equations involved. In addition, the teachers emphasize the universality of the calculation techniques; students are encouraged to believe that while they will face new equations in subsequent science and engineering courses, the calculation techniques and the algebraic manipulations will be the same. It seems clear that many learn this lesson, for in a sophomore course where the students once asked, "how should this problem be solved?", they now say, "do you care how we solve this problem?"

In this freshman engineering course, about one-fourth of the time in each class period is reserved for help with the subject matter; three-fourths of each class period is focused on the decision-making work which is expected to help the students develop confidence in their own ability to think. The level of confidence displayed by different student groups is most interesting: some lean heavily on the printed Guided Design material as if it were the "right" answer, some groups play the game by imitating the thinking process, while others are confident enough to strike out after their own unique solutions using the handouts as a guide to the decision-making process. It is interesting to note that Guided Design material appears to provide support for each type of group. Thus, at the beginning of the program when most students want to believe that the teacher has THE answer, the students follow the printed path. However, before the first term is over, every group is forced to proceed on their own to solve an unguided problem; the students mature as a result.

Does Guided Design Work?

Now that we have explained the design format of Guided Design, you surely want to know if it works. Have all these claims for Guided Design been verified by actual student performance? The answer is yes; there are data for six years of operation of the freshman engineering program at West Virginia University, which involves a sequence of two three-credit Guided Design courses. One should expect that an early focus on both single-answer problem-solving skills and the decision-making skills required to solve open-ended problems would have an impact on a student's subsequent performance in school and, as it turned out, it did. In the late 1960s, before the new freshman program began, about 37% of the students who started as freshmen in engineering at WVU graduated from the college four years later. This figure was and is close to the existing national average completion rate for large, state supported engineering schools. Many of the students who started, transferred to some other program and completed a degree at WVU, but not in engineering. However, six years later, 56% of the students began and finished the engineering program, a gain of 50% in the number of students completing the program.

This six-credit freshman Guided Design program also appears to have had a significant effect on the grade point average (GPA) of the students who graduate from engineering. It was in 1973 that the first Guided Design graduates completed their work; these students had taken the new freshman program when it was offered on an experimental basis in five classes in 1969. These 50 engineering graduates earned a GPA of 2.94, while the other engineering students who joined them at Commencement (121 who started at WVU and 42 transfer students) earned a GPA of 2.72, a difference of 0.22 in favor of the Guided Design students. Using the minimum grade point required for graduation (2.0) as a base, this meant that those students who took the freshman program earned grades that were 30% higher than the students who did not. This difference persisted in the years following 1973;

those who started at WVU and took the required two-course Guided Design sequence earned 30% better grades during their college career than those students who transferred to WVU. This difference appears to be even more meaningful when you realize that prior to 1973, those students who started at WVU had essentially the same GPA at graduation as transfer students who completed 36% of their work some-where else. We might also note that while grade inflation occurred at WVU between 1969 and 1971, is it not a factor in these data.

If you are one of those people who believes that the way you teach and test students determines the kinds of skills they develop, you should be interested in two other pieces of data. One set of data is based on the work of the chemical engineering students at WVU. In this program, the decision-making experience is continued in at least one class each semester through the sophomore, junior, and senior years. Some Guided Design is used in the sophomore year, but this quickly gives way to other forms of decision-making, includ-ing a 10-credit design course in the senior year where the stu-dents are organized as a corporate design team. These stu-dents develop much greater expertise with the decision-making process and they earn better grades. During the four years that this program has been in operation, the chemical engineering graduates have earned grades that are 21% higher than the already high grades of the other graduates from the college, a total gain of 51% in GPA.

The second piece of data describes the way one thousand graduating seniors responded to a questionnaire in 1977. When asked how they were *tested in their major*, a typical university graduate said 33.6% for facts and memorization, 44.3% equally for facts and problem-solving, and 20.9% primarily for problem-solving/analysis/creativity. A typical engineering graduate responded with 10%, 35%, 55%, while a chemical engineering graduate indicated 5.9% for facts, 0% for facts and problem-solving, and 94.1% for problem-solving/analysis/creativity.

Perhaps the best way we can sum up this description of the design format is by contrasting the Guided Design approach with that used in the operation of a more typical course. Traditional education, for example, appears to be based on the assumption that *decision-making* is a skill which can be acquired by trial and error; Guided Design is based on the belief that decision-making is a systematic process that can best be learned if the process is slowed down, the steps are identified, and specific practice is provided.

Traditional education assumes that *information acquisition* is an end in itself; Guided Design assumes that information is acquired for the purpose of making a better decision. In addition, it provides for the use of a variety of individualized instruction approaches which help students develop the skills they need to be independent learners.

The traditional system provides teachers who may *model* the role of the professional/independent-learner/decision-maker—the student is expected, but often fails to behave in a similar manner; with Guided Design the students play these roles *throughout the educational process.*

Traditional education is focused on the need for Knowledge; the Guided Design approach can develop many more, important qualities. In other words, this new educational pattern provides an appropriate way to develop the student's background for the future.

References
DESIGN FORMAT Section

Block, James H. *Mastery Learning: Theory and Practice.* New York: Holt, Rinehart, and Winston, 1971.

Maslow, A. H., *Toward a Psychology of Being*, Second Edition. New York: Van Nostrand Reinhold, 1968.

IV.

OUTCOMES

There are three kinds of observations you might make about Guided Design: what happens in class on a single day, what happens in one term, and what happens when the students' development extends through several classes. If you visit an operating Guided Design class, you will observe students discussing, interacting, agreeing, clashing, making friends (or enemies), generating ideas you would not have expected, being excited about what they're doing, involved, using the jargon of the discipline, arguing about important current issues in the discipline, challenging each other and the ideas of the profession, making use of the subject matter they studied the night before, performing experiments, recording data, and critically examining new and old ideas.

In the same class, you will observe the teacher moving from group to group, listening, asking questions, prompting, responding to student comments, reinforcing student thoughts, laughing, arguing, agreeing, clarifying confusing points in the written material (and making notes on how to correct it), and generally enjoying a challenging, professional experience.

By the end of a Guided Design course, you can expect to see students develop skills such as the following.

1. Increasingly rapid selection and sorting of pertinent information.

57

2. Increasingly sophisticated use of the decision-making steps involved; for example, the easy generation of possible solutions, rapid selection of viable alternates, more intelligent evaluation of an acceptable solution, and quick recognition and correction of errors in the solution.
3. Greater sensitivity to the surroundings and the stimuli or cues which guide thinking.

You surely recognize the development and sophistication of these skills over a long period of time in your own professional career. Tasks which seemed complex the first time you tried them (preparing a research proposal, writing a paper, giving a talk) are much easier the second time, after you develop familiarity with them. We hope the value of Guided Design, as a structured approach which can be used to develop equivalent skills in your students, is equally obvious.

Teachers using Guided Design report that student grades on subject matter examinations are better than they were previously. This gain reflects an improvement in student motivation, which usually occurs with this approach. Teachers also report other effects, such as greater perseverance, a more questioning attitude, strengthened maturity, increased verbal ability, heightened independence, and a better attitude toward their work.

Guided Design offers some important advantages over traditional educational practice, advantages that accrue to both the teacher and the students. Teachers find satisfaction in better communication, especially with beginning students, and greatly increased opportunities to talk to their students, to know their names, and to understand their backgrounds and problems. Teachers also enjoy interacting with students who know how to hold a conversation using the jargon of the discipline; they take pleasure in the students' ability to develop creative ideas that would impress their colleagues (ideas they would be glad to call their own); and in watching professional decision-making skills emerge and mature.

A further advantage for many teachers is the opportunity to develop instructional materials which better suit student needs, thereby *legitimately improving grades* and producing greater student interest in the subject matter. Gains such as these are demonstrated by the data reported in the article "Pride: A New Approach to Experiential Learning" (Bailie and Wales, 1975). Other teachers experience the feeling that they are providing both an environment and a pattern of organization which provides for the development of specific cognitive skills or intellectual operations, and the feeling that, more than ever before, they are helping students develop in ways they'd like them to develop.

An equal number of gains accrue to the students in a Guided Design course. They learn as much or more about the subject, retain what they learn longer, and *earn* better grades. They develop skills in learning to learn on their own, communicating with other students and with faculty, logical thinking, and decision-making. One research study showed, for example, that one semester of Guided Design significantly increased the students' Internal Orientation with regard to Locus of Control and lowered the students' Manifest Anxiety (Tseng and Wales, 1972).

As pointed out earlier, the concept of Guided Design is built on an eclectic integration of psychological viewpoints. It includes modeling, practice, advance organizers, and competency-based testing and reinforcement, to name a few. It also provides an environment where each of the items on Maslow's "Need Hierarchy" can be satisfied. For example, the need for *Self-actualization* is satisfied by a constant focus on *Decision-Making*. Small-group discussions of open-ended problems provide a setting where students can explore and develop personal beliefs. These problems not only establish

a need for the *Knowledge* and *Values* each student is expected to learn, but also they provide a reason for learning.
The use of competency-based testing and other new teaching-
learning activities helps the student learn more of what is
expected. In addition, an individualized approach to instruction allows the student to gain the needed *Respect* and self-
respect. These needs can also be satisfied through the group
work, where the student has an opportunity to contribute
to the discussion. Furthermore, the group provides an environment where the student's need for *Belonging* can be
satisfied. The use of PSI, competency, and new approaches
increases the *Safety* for the student's efforts. And the development of decision-making skills contributes to the student's ability to satisfy the *Self-preservation* need after
school is over.

Those teachers who prefer a cognitive base for their work
should also find merit in Guided Design, for it is built upon
ideas like those presented in Bloom's *Taxonomy of Educational Objectives: Cognitive Domain*. The three highest levels
in the *Taxonomy*, analysis, synthesis, and evaluation, are key
steps in open-ended problem-solving because they are usually
required to perform any of the other steps. For instance, to
gather information, a student must analyze his or her needs;
synthesize or gather the information from the library, other
people, or experiments; and then evaluate what has been ob-
tained to determine if it is adequate. With Guided Design,
teachers can help students learn to perform these steps and
observe the skill they bring to the performance. The same is
true for the lower levels in the *Taxonomy*. Teachers can
transmit information about Knowledge or Values to the
students and determine how well they are able to respond to
single-answer homework and/or test problems which require
them to use one of the Intellectual Abilities, i.e., to recall,
manipulate, translate, interpret, predict, or choose.

Although the issue addressed by Guided Design is a new focus on decision-making, a serendipitous effect is an improved treatment of subject matter and a corresponding improvement in student learning. There are two aspects to this gain in learning. Part of the gain is produced by coupling the subject matter to the solution of a series of open-ended problems. Each project is designed to establish a legitimate need for some of the facts, concepts, and values the students are expected to learn. You might say the students "discover" a need to learn new material, but in fact they arrive at this discovery because the teacher planned it. This does not mean the students will see a need for all the detailed concepts and principles they study. In fact, they will probably learn more than they need to know and not use all that is learned. However, they will do this willingly if the project provides them with a clearcut reason to want to study the general subject matter area.

Since students use at least part of what they have learned to solve each problem, their retention of subject matter concepts is significantly improved. This is in sharp contrast to some courses, where the relevance of the material may not always be obvious; and, according to psychologists, students may well forget up to 80 percent of what has been "learned" within a few weeks of the examination—after the need to know is past.

A second important reason for an observable gain in student learning is the work the teacher does to insure that students can learn on their own outside of class. Of the many examples we could cite to demonstrate this development, we have chosen three. One is from a multi-disciplinary course titled "The Nature of Evidence," which uses Guided Design to help students learn to compare and contrast the way in which professionals from the humanities, social sciences, and natural sciences gather evidence and make decisions. What the faculty who designed this course learned is that a single key word could make a great difference in the students' understanding of a concept. They learned this because the students had to use what they studied outside of class as a base for the decision-making work in class where the teacher could observe their behavior. When the students couldn't intelligently take a step, the faculty knew something was wrong with the self-study material (or their Guided Design material).

When a defect is discovered, the teacher probes the students with questions to see if the specific problem can be identified. When it is, the teacher may give a "mini-lecture" to provide the needed guidance. Then, at the end of the class, the material is revised and replaced. The amount of repair required is sometimes amazing, but the net result is greatly improved student learning.

A second example of material improvement comes from an engineering course where freshman students were expected to learn how to perform "thermodynamics" calculations on their own. This learning was supported by carefully drawn models presented in linear programmed instruction form (Wales, Stager, and Long, 1974). It was discovered that while the students learned how to do the calculations, their approach was disorganized and sloppy. This problem was corrected by the addition of three branched programs which taught the strategy of single-answer problem-solving.

The final example is drawn from the experience of the chemical engineering teachers who used Guided Design in a sophomore level course. Class time had formerly been used to help students develop the skills needed to identify and solve a set of simultaneous equations, i.e., to perform material balance calculations. No existing textbook presented these concepts well enough to support self-study, so the teachers developed both linear and branched programmed material (Wales, Bailie, and Pappano, 1974). In the process of developing and revising this material, the teachers developed some innovative methods of problem analysis and attack which helped students handle formerly difficult concepts with ease. As in each of the other cases, there was an observable gain in what the students learned.

You can help students develop decision-making skills in a variety of ways; simulations, games, case studies, and internships are all excellent examples. Guided Design offers a unique advantage over other approaches, particularly when inexperienced decision-makers are involved, because it is built on carefully drawn models which help build the students' confidence by providing step by step support, a decision-making structure, and a good deal of practice. In addition, Guided Design is built upon written materials. A key aspect of written materials is that they can be criticized by both colleagues and students. This gives the teacher the feedback needed to correct faults in the design. Many teachers have learned, for example, that writing out the solution to an open-ended problem avoids a great deal of confusion.

The problem that occurs when a teacher tries to lead students through an unstructured discussion is not that the teacher fails to model the decision-making process, but rather that the model is too sophisticated. Thus, as a result of previous experience, the teacher might combine steps, skip steps, rearrange steps, integrate steps, and automatically recycle through steps. In addition, the teacher might not verbalize some of the steps involved, such as identifying the real problem, and fail to state key assumptions, constraints, or facts. The student who is trying to learn by this process has two problems—the problem to be solved and the problem of figuring out what the teacher is doing. At best, the student can learn only part of the model being demonstrated. In addition, the discussion has the weakness of being temporal; once the words have been said—once the action has been completed—it is gone, and the memory of the student is the only basis for reconstructing what has occurred. Written materials help solve this problem Even the student who was absent from a class has some guidance—the printed Instructions and Feedback to use as a basis for review and learning.

The advantages of Guided Design increase in direct proportion to a teacher's interest in helping students develop decision-making skills. Guided Design provides both a plan and a vehicle which make it possible for teachers to achieve this goal in their classroom. If the adoption involves more than one course, for example a sequence of courses in a department, there are additional gains because several teachers can plan both the subject matter organization and the intellectual development of the student more completely. One such application, in a four-year chemical engineering program, made it possible to direct students toward appropriate reference material in early course work, use fewer prompts as the students became familiar with available material, and then to observe their behavior in later courses to see if the proper development did occur. If it does not, the system can be redesigned until requisite skills are generated.

References
(OUTCOMES Section)

Bailie, R. C., and Wales, C. E. Pride: A New Approach to Experiential Learning. *Engineering Education*, Vol. 65, No. 5, February 1975.

Tseng, M. S., and Wales, C. E. Effect of a Guided Design Course Pattern on Student Personality Variables. *Engineering Education*, Vol. 62, No. 7, April 1972.

Wales, C. E., Stager, R. A., and Long, T. R. *Guided Engineering Design.* St. Paul, Minn.: West Publishing Co., 1974.

Wales, C. E., Bailie, R. C., and Pappano, A. W. *Physical and Chemical Material Balance Calculations*, Chemical Engineering Department, West Virginia University, 1974.

V.

DEVELOPMENTAL GUIDE

If you decide to adopt Guided Design, you must be prepared to invest some time either locating materials that fit your needs, or preparing your own projects. If you do locate appropriate materials, the only other task required is to familiarize yourself with how to operate the class, which might involve visiting an operating class or attending a workshop.

If you prefer to develop your own material, there are several paths you might follow. One would be to prepare a script for your project and to talk the students through the problem. One faculty member took this approach in a Spanish department. To get quick, multiple tests of his work, he volunteered to fill-in for any colleague who was ill or going out of town. In two weeks he had a script covered with the creative responses of the students and more than enough material to develop an excellent written project.

A second path would be to use the introductory material presented in this book and prepare a single project of your own for any portion of your course where adequate subject matter materials exist. If you decide to go further and develop materials for a whole course, you may need three, four or five projects. The first project is usually the most sophisticated and complete; less material and guidance may be required in each succeeding project. In a one-semester drama history course, for example, six projects were prepared, but the last one was simply a one-page statement which served as the base for a take-home final on the decision-making work. In the Nature of Evidence course, four projects are used; while a freshman engineering course involves only three projects per term.

The teacher who decides to adopt Guided Design and prepare original materials for a complete course may face two creative tasks. One is the preparation of the Instruction-Feedback project material, the other is the preparation of support materials. It does take time to create a set of projects which communicate the logic of decision-making. The number of hours required depends, of course, on how well you write and organize. But the job gets easier after you clear the hurdle of the first project and develop your own style.

The work that remains might include the preparation of objectives, study guides, and/or notes to support the out-of-class work of the students. Eventually, you might also want to prepare homework problems and competency-based tests. However, none of these support materials are required to adopt Guided Design (although we highly recommend them as part of a complete package of teaching-learning-testing activities). A "Procedural Guide" which can help you organize this effort is given below.

PROCEDURAL GUIDE: GUIDED DESIGN

	Project			
	A	B	C	D
1. Choose the *subject matter* you expect the students to learn during the project. (Think in terms of the reading or viewing assignments you plan to give them.)				

Project

	A	B	C	D

2. Select an *open-ended problem* situation which will lead to a need for some of this subject matter.

3. *Outline* the project. (You might use 3x5 cards with one card for each step in the decision-making process.)
   a. Write a one or two line statement of the *goal* of the professional's work.
   b. Identify some of the *information* that should be gathered.
   c. List two or three *possible solutions* that might be used.
   d. State a few *constraints* that apply to this situation.
   e. Identify the *"best solution."*
   f. List the key elements that should be considered in the *analysis*.

4. *Write* the Instruction-Feedback material for your project. This is a high-level creative task, so it is not easy to provide guidance via written words. What you are about to write is a narrative or story which does two things:
   a. It describes the work of some person or group who are actually solving a problem. Your students will be asked to play this role.
   b. It leads the students through each of the steps in your outline, asking them to make their own decision before they receive your feedback on what a professional would have done.

5. Select the specific resources and pages the students should study and list these in a *Reading Assignment*.

6. List the *Objectives* for the project including both decision-making and subject matter objectives.

7. Convert the objectives into a set of *Homework* problems and prepare an answer to each problem.

	Project			
	A	**B**	**C**	**D**
8. Prepare the *Parallel Project* assignment sheet.				
9. *Add* homework or reading assignment reminders to the appropriate Instruction-Feedback step in the project.				
10. Prepare *Quizzes* or *Examinations* for both the project work and subject matter.				
11. Type, print, and punch the material.				
12. *Teach* your class.				

Enough teachers of a variety of persuasions have adopted Guided Design so that we can honestly claim that it is not a particularly complex innovation. The prime cost involved is related to the teacher time required to develop materials. Some faculty have prepared and tested Guided Design project material while teaching a normal load of classes. Others have had released time to do a more complete job, which is clearly the preferred arrangement. Additional related costs involve typing and reproducing new materials. Some outside consultant help may be required until the on-site teacher gets a feel for the organization of the system and develops experience preparing project materials, but many teachers have done all this work on their own.

Since the key element in the development of a Guided Design course is an investment of teacher time, we want to describe four ways in which this time might be invested.

First, teachers must understand the logic of Guided Design. We hope this presentation provides the basic insight that is required, but, as we said earlier, a visit to an operating class would be a desirable addition because it is difficult to communicate the "art" of teaching via a book. Those who want additional background on the "science" of pertinent educational principles can read four or five of the references we have recommended; in most cases these are short paperback books. Perhaps it is worth noting at this point that most of the teachers who have prepared materials, implemented classes, and successfully operated Guided Design courses have not had any special training in either psychology or education.

Second, teachers must invest time preparing project material. Some teachers have independently prepared excellent material for their own course. Others, especially those working in a discipline where no model projects exist, have required help from someone who has had experience in developing or polishing project materials. Depending on the writing ability of the teacher, the *initial* draft of the materials for a project for nine, 50-minute class sessions might take from 10 to 20 hours to prepare. After constructive criticism, it may take an additional five hours to rewrite the materials. However, a teacher who has had some experience with this process should take less time to develop additional materials. Furthermore, in some classes highly detailed Instruction-Feedback material is only required for the first two or three projects in a sequence.

Third, the teacher may need time to develop self-study materials which students can use to learn subject matter concepts outside of class. Even if a good textbook exists, some time may be required to prepare objectives, a study guide, and homework questions. If lectures have been necessary in the past to clarify what is in the text, it may take time to prepare an equivalent set of notes. If no adequate text material exists, it may require *a good deal of time* to prepare, test, and revise programmed instruction, audio-tutorial materials, or some other self-study support system. If adequate

support does not exist, the preparation of this material undoubtedly represents the biggest constraint on the development of a system.

Fourth, before a class of students starts their first Guided
Design project they must be prepared for this new type of
teaching-learning experience. As we said earlier, the new pattern of operation should be explained to the students so they
do not develop anxieties which will subvert what you are
trying to accomplish. Unless the teacher decides to use one of
the existing introductions, time will be needed to develop
this introductory material.

An individual teacher can apply this technique to a course
—and many have. However, we have found great value in the
interactive criticism provided by a team of two or more people who work together to develop materials. In fact, many of
the operating systems have been developed by a small team
of two to four teachers. If your department decides to build
a thread of decision-making work through a series of courses,
the workload decreases, because less and less material is
needed as the students' abilities evolve.

Two constraints you may face if you adopt Guided Design
are student resistance to a new idea and operating problems
such as space and class size. Students behave like people—
they resist change. If students have been successful through
12 or more years of previous education, they are not likely to
welcome a new pattern of operation. Students also tend to
focus on grades, and once they know how to get the grades
they want, they don't like someone changing the rules of the
game. You can help overcome this resistance by thoroughly
explaining what you are trying to do and by using competency-based testing, which reduces the threat of low grades
by allowing students to retest and earn a good grade if they
are willing to work for it.

Space is another constraint you must consider when you

plan your course. Guided Design operates best in a room where students can work together around small tables. Tablet arm chairs pulled in a circle will do almost as well, but fixed or tiered seats are not likely to be a successful setting. You also need more space than would otherwise be required for the same number of students, because they are talking to each other within their groups and you should avoid noise interference between groups.

One of the most important operating constraints you must consider is that of class size. Back in the early 1800's, each college teacher worked intimately with five or six students— education was based on the European model which had served so well. But the "Land-Grant Act" changed all that when it created "mass" education. As enrollments grew, we lost sight of the fact that the teacher could no longer talk and work with a few students. One attempt to recapture what was lost is the whole class discussion, but this does not provide the practice each student needs to develop ethics, values, subject matter, and decision-making skills. A better solution, from our viewpoint, is the one chosen for Guided Design, where groups of four or five students make a daily contribution and get feedback from peers. However, if a class is too large, it still reduces the possibility for interaction between the teacher and groups.

VI.

RESOURCES

If you decide to convert your course to Guided Design, you may find some published material useful. We see four possibilities. First, you may find that someone has developed a whole set of Guided Design projects which suits your needs. Second, you may discover one or more projects which fit your course requirements and thus reduce the amount of writing you have to do. Third, some available project material may be useful if modified slightly by the addition of a few pages which adapt it to your subject matter plans. And fourth, the material you obtain may simply serve as a model of the Guided Design style for your own writing. Decision-making, after all, is relatively independent of discipline and you are likely to find that a spectrum of examples from different fields is more helpful than one or two examples from your own area.

BOOKS
1. Wales, C. E., and Stager, R. A. *Guided Design*, available from C. E. Wales, Freshman Engineering, at West Virginia University, 1977. This book has been the starting point for most faculty who decide to adopt Guided Design.

2. Wales, C. E., Stager, R. A., and Long, T. R. *Guided Engineering Design: Project Book.* St. Paul, Minn.: West Publishing Co., 1974. Projects for a first course in engineering.

3. D'Amour, G., and Wales, C. E. (ed.) *The Nature of Evidence,* available from G. D'Amour, Philosophy Department at West Virginia University, 1976. Individual Guided Design projects are available from this book, which serves a multidisciplinary course. The projects include the following: (1) "An Introduction to Decision-Making" and "An Introduction to the Problem of Evidence," (2) Philosophy, (3) Physics, (4) Anthropology, (5) Geology, (6) Political Science, (7) English, (8) Psychology, (9) Chemistry, and (10) Drama.

4. D'Amour, G. Teaching Philosophy by the Guided Design Method. *Teaching Philosophy Today: Criticism and Response.* Schenectady, N.Y.: National Information and Resource Center for the Teaching of Philosophy, 1976.

5. Projects for a graduate level program in counseling and rehabilitation can be ordered from the department office, 502 Allen Hall, WVU.

6. Those interested in chemical engineering can order material from Professor Richard Bailie at WVU. This includes projects for a sophomore class and texts on *Physical and Chemical Material Balance Calculations* and *Energy-Material Balance Calculations.*

ARTICLES

1. Wales, Charles E., and Stager, Robert A. The Design of an Educational System. *Engineering Education,* Vol. 62, No. 5, February 1972.

2. Stager, Robert A., and Wales, Charles E. Guided Design: A New Concept in Course Design and Operation. *Engineering Education*, Vol. 62, No. 6, March 1972.

3. Feldhusen, John F., Guided Design: An Evaluation of the Course and Course Pattern. *Engineering Education*, Vol. 62, No. 6, March 1972.

4. Tseng, M. A., and Wales, C. E. Effect of a Guided Design Course Pattern on Student Personality Variables. *Engineering Education*, Vol. 62, No. 7, April 1972.

5. Sherren, David C. Design and Evaluation of an Instructional Unit in Technical Report Writing. *Engineering Education*, Vol. 62, No. 7, April 1972.

6. Wales, Charles E. Guided Design: Why and How You Should Use It. *Engineering Education*, Vol. 62, No. 8, May 1972.

7. Colvin, Samuel T., Kilmer, Douglas A., and Smith, James E. Guided Design in Environmental Education. *Engineering Education*, Vol. 62, No. 8, May 1972.

8. Masson, Robert L. Prescription: Guided Decision Making. *Engineering Education*, Vol. 62, No. 8, May 1972.

9. Stager, R. A. Guided-Design. *Media Message*, 4, #1, pp. 16-23 (Fall, 1974). The Association for Media and Technology in Education in Canada, Queens U, Kingston, Ontario.

10. Bailie, R. C., and Wales, C. E. PRIDE: A New Approach to Experiential Learning. *Engineering Education*, Vol. 65, No. 5, February 1975.

11. Goldberg, F. M., and D'Amour, G. Integrating Physics and the Philosophy of Science Through Guided Design. *American Journal of Physics*, Vol. 44, No. 9, September 1976.

12. Wales, C. E. Programmed Instruction to Guided Design. *NSPI Newsletter*, Vol. XII, No. 5, June 1973.

Kathy,

Could we get this film for learning workshop — 7-23 → 7-24

D'Amour. Many seminars and talks have also been given.

PROJECTS IN USE

If you want additional help, you are likely to find that many of the people who have developed Guided Design projects are willing to share their effort with you. Some of those we know have used this approach are listed below.

Business—Walter Kramer, Portland State University, Oregon; Gregory P. White, Loyola University of Chicago; Matt Amano, Oregon State University; Peter Newsted, University of Manitoba; Karen S. Burn, New Mexico State University, Las Cruces.

Education—John Feldhusen and Russell Ames, Purdue University; Jean Morse, Medical College of Georgia-Augusta; William Russell, Merrimack College, Mass.; James Hale, Portland State University; Stephan J. Clarke, Salem State College, Mass.; Thomas Woodrow, Juniata College, Pa.; David Srebalus and Thomas Lombardi, West Virginia University; Sister Mary Edward Dolan, Clarke College, Iowa; Patricia Smith and Tom Hatcher, West Virginia University; Paul DeLargy, Valdosta State College, Georgia; George Hadley, Idaho State University, Pocatello, Idaho.

2. Stager, Robert A., and Wales, Charles E. Guided Design: A New Concept in Course Design and Operation. *Engineering Education*, Vol. 62, No. 6, March 1972.

3. Feldhusen, John F., Guided Design: An Evaluation of the Course and Course Pattern. *Engineering Education*, Vol. 62, No. 6, March 1972.

4. Tseng, M. A., and Wales, C. E. Effect of a Guided Design Course Pattern on Student Personality Variables. *Engineering Education*, Vol. 62, No. 7, April 1972.

5. Sherren, David C. Design and Evaluation of an Instructional Unit in Technical Report Writing. *Engineering Education*, Vol. 62, No. 7, April 1972.

6. Wales, Charles E. Guided Design: Why and How You Should Use It. *Engineering Education*, Vol. 62, No. 8, May 1972.

7. Colvin, Samuel T., Kilmer, Douglas A., and Smith, James E. Guided Design in Environmental Education. *Engineering Education*, Vol. 62, No. 8, May 1972.

8. Masson, Robert L. Prescription: Guided Decision Making. *Engineering Education*, Vol. 62, No. 8, May 1972.

9. Stager, R. A. Guided-Design. *Media Message*, 4, #1, pp. 16-23 (Fall, 1974). The Association for Media and Technology in Education in Canada, Queens U, Kingston, Ontario.

10. Bailie, R. C., and Wales, C. E. PRIDE: A New Approach to Experiential Learning. *Engineering Education*, Vol. 65, No. 5, February 1975.

11. Goldberg, F. M., and D'Amour, G. Integrating Physics and the Philosophy of Science Through Guided Design. *American Journal of Physics*, Vol. 44, No. 9, September 1976.

12. Wales, C. E. Programmed Instruction to Guided Design. *NSPI Newsletter*, Vol. XII, No. 5, June 1973.

FILM

The Exxon Education Foundation has produced a film about Guided Design. This film is now available on free loan for faculty groups, seminars, classes, etc. To order the film, write: Film Scheduling Center, Modern Talking Picture Service, Inc., 2323 New Hyde Park Rd., New Hyde Park, N.Y. 11040; Tel: (516) 488-3810.

WORKSHOPS

Over 50 two-day workshops have been given in the U.S.A. and in other countries by Dr. Wales, Dr. Stager, and/or Dr. D'Amour. Many seminars and talks have also been given.

PROJECTS IN USE

If you want additional help, you are likely to find that many of the people who have developed Guided Design projects are willing to share their effort with you. Some of those we know have used this approach are listed below.

Business—Walter Kramer, Portland State University, Oregon; Gregory P. White, Loyola University of Chicago; Matt Amano, Oregon State University; Peter Newsted, University of Manitoba; Karen S. Burn, New Mexico State University, Las Cruces.

Education—John Feldhusen and Russell Ames, Purdue University; Jean Morse, Medical College of Georgia-Augusta; William Russell, Merrimack College, Mass.; James Hale, Portland State University; Stephan J. Clarke, Salem State College, Mass.; Thomas Woodrow, Juniata College, Pa.; David Srebalus and Thomas Lombardi, West Virginia University; Sister Mary Edward Dolan, Clarke College, Iowa; Patricia Smith and Tom Hatcher, West Virginia University; Paul DeLargy, Valdosta State College, Georgia; George Hadley, Idaho State University, Pocatello, Idaho.

Chemistry—Roland Schulz, Oklahoma Christian College; Horace Jackson, Purdue University.

Physical Science—Gerald O'Brien, Mount Wachusett Community College, Mass.; C. H. Hinricks, Linfield College, Oregon.

Mathematics—Jerry Goldman, DePaul University-Chicago; Joe E. Lingerfelt, Northern Arizona University; Dennis Ebersole, Northampton County Area Community College, Pa.

Biology—John L. Zimmerman, Kansas State University.

Engineering—Chor Weng Tan, The Cooper Union (freshman); Edward Tillamn, University of Bridgeport (ME); Edwin Clark, Clemson University (CE); Ron Eck, West Virginia University (CE); John Webster, University of Wisconsin (EE); Ronald K. Shepler, Alderson Broaddus College (freshman).

Multidisciplinary Studies—Mary Brown, Knoxville College; Barry Lipscomb, Virginia Weslyan College; Janet Lewis, Juniata College; Vernon L. Simula, University of Minnesota-Duluth; Roderick Davis, City University of New York, John Jay College of Criminal Justice.

Social Studies—William L. Crozier, Saint Mary's College, Winona, Minn. (American Studies); Isaiah McIver, Savannah State College (World History); Lloyd Jensen, Temple University (International Relations); Ted Hiser, Cleveland State University (Urban Studies); Thomas Woodrow, Juniata College (American History); Parker G. Marden, St. Lawrence University (Sociology of Alcohol Abuse); Robert Crowley, Sangamon State University (Midwestern City); David Rafky, Biscayne College (Criminal Justice); David Lawrence, Westmont College (American Politics); Frances Smith, S. D. Bishop Junior College, Alabama (Honors Program); Paul Friedman, University of Kansas (Human Relations); Mark Toltan, North Carolina Central University, Durham (Economics); John Finn, Goucher College, Towsan, Maryland (Psychology).

Professional and Graduate—David Samuel and Edwin Michael, West Virginia University (Wildlife Management); James Applegate, Rutgers University (Wildlife Management); Gordon L. Coppic, Purdue University (Veterinary Pharmacology); Helen Jordan, Oklahoma State University (Physiological Sciences); T. M. Hammonds, Oregon State University (Agricultural Economics); Virginia Hagemann and Debbie Harr, West Virginia University (Nursing); Jan Kennedy, Alverno College (Library Science); William B. Kemp, Medical College of Virginia (Endodontics Seminar); Arlene L. Fraikor, University of Kansas School of Medicine, Wichita Campus (Integral Health).

CHARLES E. WALES is professor of Engineering and Education and Director of Freshman Engineering at West Virginia University. His work as an "educational engineer" resulted in the development of a new teaching-learning approach called Guided Design. He and Robert A. Stager have published a book titled *Guided Design*, which describes this innovation and serves as the basis for workshops on the subject. With others, he has also developed books for a first course in engineering, *Guided Engineering Design*, and a multidisciplinary course, *The Nature of Evidence*.

This work has been recognized by a variety of teaching awards including the ASEE-George Westinghouse Award. The Guided Design concept is one of four selected by the Exxon Education Foundation for promotion in their "Impact" grants program, which has helped spread the use of this approach throughout the country in science, social science, humanities, and professional courses.

ROBERT A. STAGER, a Canadian by birth, was educated in both Canada (to an M.A.Sc. in Chemical Engineering, Toronto) and in the U.S.A. (Ph.D., Illinois). For the last 13 years he has been a professor in Chemical Engineering at the University of Windsor. For three years he served as department head.

Dr. Stager co-developed Guided Design during a creative sabbatical at West Virginia University. The results of this effort include a freshman engineering textbook and two texts on developing Guided Design systems. He has further conveyed the concept of Guided Design by published articles, oral presentations, and workshops.

In recent years at Windsor, he has been a co-developer and administrator of a freshman engineering design and computations course. In all these efforts, he has been committed to the "hows" and "whys" of small-group learning.